Sweet Rhymes
for
Sweet Hearts

By
Debasish Mridha, M.D.
Illustrations by Gil Balbuena Jr.

To order additional copies of this book, contact:
Xlibris LLC
1-888-795-4274
www.Xlibris.com
Orders@Xlibris.com

Dancing with Daddy

My little heart, my little girl.
Dance with Daddy; dance, my pearl.
Hold my hand; dance with your feet.
Sing a little song; dance with the beat.
Dance with a smile; sing with joy.
Dance like a peacock; sing like a toy.
Dance with love; sing with kindness.
Life will be blissful, full of happiness.
Dance with Daddy; dance, my pearl.
My little heart, my little girl.

Morning Song

I am a glowing morning sun.
I give light; I am bright.
I am quiet and very fun.
I am a beautiful morning bird.
I am singing; I am dancing.
I can be a wise nerd.
I am a gentle morning breeze.
I am tickling; I am touching.
I am playing with the trees.

School Friends

I like to read; reading is cool.
I like to dance; I love school.
I like to sing; singing is fun.
I like to run in the morning sun.
I like my friend; a friend is a joy.
We play together with our favorite toy.

Rain or Shine

Rainy day or sunny day,
Having fun anyway.
The sun and clouds play all day,
The sun is hiding at the bay.
I am playing in the falling rain.
The sun is shining again and again.
I love the sun and I love the rain.
The sun is fun and the rain can entertain.

Rainbow

I draw a rainbow with seven colors of ink.
Red, orange, yellow, green
Blue, purple, and pink.
I love my rainbow.
Looks like a real bow.
Hangs in the sky.
Can't touch, it's too high.
It paints the evening sky.
At night, rainbow says bye-bye.

The Best Day

Come out girls; come out boys.
We will run and play with toys.
It is morning; the sun is rising.
Birds are singing; birds are dancing.
We will dance; we will play.
We will have fun all day.
Today is a sunny day; it is a play day.
Today is a holiday; it is the best day.

Dancing Band

We are dancing; we are singing.
We are holding hands.
We are rounding; we are bending.
We are forming bands.
We are joyful; we are cheerful.
We are falling on the ground.
We are dancing; we are singing.
We are making a joyful sound.

My Lovely Cat

Curly, pearly, my cat,
Likes to play with the rat.
Meow, *meow*; likes to sing.
Likes to jump; *ding, ding.*

She is a lovely cat.
She loves when I pat.
She is very smart.
She is a living art.

In the Daytime

We will make a pancake in the morning.
We will pat-a-cake in the evening.
We will cook dinner in the afternoon.
We will make our lunch at noon.
We will do homework with our mommy.
We will play a fun game with our daddy.
We will recite a rhyme at school time.
We will read a story at bedtime.

Sharing and Caring

You are my friend.
You follow the trend.
I like to play with you
When I get time to.
I like to share with you
My toys and my glue.
You are very gentle and kind.
You are always on my mind.

Little Feet Dancing

Dance, dance, dance with little feet.
Lift little hands; sing a little beat.
Dance, little baby, dance with me.
Hold my hand and sing like a bee.
Dance with Daddy; dance with Mommy.
Dance with joy; dance like Tommy.
Dance, little baby, dance with me.
Hold my hand and sing like a bee.

Morning

This is morning, beautiful morning.
The sun is shining bright.
Wind is blowing; the leaves are dancing.
The birds are singing just right.

At the Beach

At the beach, I was playing
With my toys, in the sand.
At the beach, I was singing
With my friend and with the band.
At the beach, I was laughing
With my joy and wondering mind.
At the beach, I was running
To see the beauty and be very kind.

Dancing Squirrel

I saw a squirrel dancing on a tree.
Snow was on the ground; he was not free.
He was jumping from one branch to another.
Searching for food to quiet his hunger.
He was washing his face again and again.
Calling his friend by scratching his brain.
It was very cold and he was waiting for the sun.
I love to watch squirrels; they are real fun.

Swimming

Cool pool in the school.
Water is clean and cool.
I like to swim in the pool.
Swimming is fun and cool.
To be the best in school,
Be cool and follow the rule.

Playing the Day Away

Rainy day, sunny day, funny day is today.
Sometimes rain, sometimes shine in the bay.
Anyway, we will play all day
In the cold, in the rain, in the bay.

Everyday

Sunday is a nothing day.
Monday is a busy day.
Tuesday is an easy day.
Wednesday is a lazy day.
Thursday is a funny day.
Friday is a singing day.
Saturday is a playing day.
I love every day.
Every day is the best day.

Months and Seasons

January, February, March,
It is winter and it is very cold.
April, May, June,
It is spring and it is bright gold.
July, August, September,
It is summer and it is wonderful.
October, November, December,
It is fall and it is colorful.

Dancing Snowflakes

Tickling, prickling snowflakes
Touching, melting on the lakes.
Flying, dancing in the air.
Falling, hiding in my hair.
Writing, drawing beautiful art
On my window, in my heart.
Tickling, prickling snowflakes,
I love them like ice cream cakes.

Sweet Rhymes for Sweet Hearts

Boys and girls, come together.
We will have fun, dance together.
We will sing like a singing bird.
We will dance like a little herd.
We will dance holding each other's hand.
We will form a little singing band.
We will have joy; we will have fun.
We will smile like the morning sun.
Everyone will enjoy our sweet rhyme
For sweet hearts, for a lifetime.